Your Powerful
To The Point
Book

I0170103

She Saved Me

Choosing Joy After a Tragedy

By
Diana Collins

Next Stage Communications
3638 Tioga Way
Las Vegas, NV 89169
(702) 682-8431

ISBN: **978-1-7338602-1-5**

Dedication:

To Sabrina:
Thank you for always watching over me. I'll see you on the other side but not anytime soon, I promise!

To Genevieve and Teresa:
My sweet girls. Thank you for letting me be your mommy! You are the two reasons why I fight to be the best mom I can be for you. Mommy loves you, Genny bean and T-Rex!

To Daniel:
My love, even after everything we've been through, you never gave up on me and continue to show me the beauty you see in me! Thank you for always loving me even during the darkest times. You are my light.

To Angie, Rosie, Keith, Grandma Chela, & Aunt Jackie:
I'm sad and sorry that we share the same loss and I can't imagine the pain you still feel. I want to thank you for loving me as if I am a part of the family. I hope I continue to make you proud by keeping Sabrina's memory alive. I love you all dearly!

To Sarah, Lindsay, Jessica, and Erica:
My PPD Sisters! You have helped The Always with Me Foundation become an actual nonprofit! I couldn't have done it without you. Thank you for pushing me and being my friend when all I wanted was to give up. I love you forever

Table of Contents

INTRODUCTION

March 07, 2019

Dear Sabrina,

Life has never been the same since you've been gone. It's been three years, and the hurt is still here. Maybe not as bad but it will always be there. I know you hate to see me hurt. That is why I have dedicated my life to you. I am living a life worth living! You see, somehow even with you being gone, you've found a way to save me! Throughout this whole grieving journey, you've shown me a life of empathy and joy. You've taught me to be happy because we only get one chance! So why wait for the "right" time to do anything when that right time is NOW!

Sabrina, you've given me strength and courage.

Something I never knew I had. Thank you for saving

me!

I love you forever.

Your best friend,

Diana

We Are Too Young To Say Goodbye Like This

I was seven months pregnant on March 4th, 2016 and my phone goes off in the middle of the night. It's 4 AM, and I thought, "Who could be texting me at this hour?" It was my friend Jackie, whom I've known since grade school. As I look over to my phone, I notice the buzz was from a facebook notification. I open up the application and find that I was tagged in a photo. It was an old photo of Sabrina, Rachel, Jackie, and me. All of my girlfriends from high school! The photo instantly put a smile on my face and I remember a time we all once had together. I missed them so much and our friendship. My joy suddenly turns into shock when look at the caption, and all I can see is "Rest in

Peace." I freeze, and my heart falls to the ground. Who is Jackie talking about? It couldn't have been Rachel because I just saw her post something on Facebook! Something told me it was Sabrina and everything in my body goes numb. I turn over to my left to wake up my husband, Daniel. I scream, "She's gone! Daniel, She's gone! Sabrina is gone! She's dead!" Right away, I try to play detective and try to figure out what is going on. Daniel wakes up and holds me. All of this feels like a total nightmare!

I had an hour before I had to get ready for work and I find myself searching for answers. I did not have Sabrina's family on my Facebook, and I wasn't able to find any answers. My heart is racing! What's happening? Where are her children? Is everyone ok? I needed answers. For a second my mind goes to the last time I spoke with her which was in November of 2015.

We were having a conversation at night just talking about our struggles. We ended our chat with an, "I love you, and I'll see you soon." Little did I know that that would be the last time I would ever hear from her again. By knowing how Sabrina tends to act over the years when she is in a bad place, she tends to remove herself from her friends. It was February 2016, and I thought, "Gee, I have not talked to Sabrina in a while, let me send her a text." She never replied, and I thought nothing of it. I later found out that around that time, she was struggling and have faced multiple suicide attempts. Till this day, I still wished I had known something. Could that conversation in November be her call for help? Did I miss the signs? Was I a crappy friend for not reaching out sooner? Should I have called her instead? My friends and family would always remind me that there was nothing

I could have done, but it will take me some time to believe that truth.

The day continues, and Daniel and I drive to work that morning. I don't know how I was able to get dressed and managed to put mascara on. Later that morning I ended up sending Sabrina's sister Angie a message on Facebook since that was the only way I knew how to get a hold of her. I felt guilty as if I didn't deserve to know but, I was her best friend, and if there was going to be a funeral, I deserved to be there. After much hesitation, I finally press send, and the message was simple. I send her my condolences first, and I ask her what happened. Of course, she did not answer right away. No one had to tell me how much her family was hurting. Sabrina had a huge family, and without even talking to them, I felt their pain. So, I would have understood if she didn't reply for a couple of days. My mind is all over the place, and I am having a hard time trying to keep my focus on work. An hour goes by, and I hear my phone make a noise. It was a Facebook message. I thought, "That must be Angie!" My heart is beating a million miles per minute.

Can I handle knowing the truth? I pick up my phone and open the message. It was indeed Angie, and she sends me the most transparent and straightforward message. It read, "Sabrina hung herself. I am so sorry." My assumptions were right, but I had no clue she would do something like that. That image of her in her last hour stayed on my mind for months. Although I was not the one who found her, that image haunted me for a very long time. Why Sabrina? Why didn't you reach out? Why didn't you call me? She knew I would have been there for her at the drop of a hat.

So many emotions run through my head that

day. I was angry with her because of how she left her daughters behind. I was sad because her daughters will not grow up with their mother and as a mother of a daughter, that pain hit too close to home. Then, the guilt started to sink in. I was the one friend that knew her struggles, should I have done more? I felt all of these emotions run right through me. Never in my life have I ever felt this way. I've experienced death yes. I lost my Aunt Diane in 2011 from breast cancer, and that loss brought much pain. Of course, I still think about her today. I also lost a co-worker when I was just 16, and he was in his 20s. We were not all that close, but I remember being at his wake feeling the emotions of grief. However, this was something much more. Sabrina and I were getting closer as friends, we've watched each other grow into motherhood; we were also mothers to daughters. This whole thing hit way too close to home! I felt like time was taken away from me. I'm also so angry because Sabrina and I just started working on our friendship and now she's gone? She was my only mom friend that I could say I grew up with and now she's gone? Why? Why couldn't I have a little more time with her? It just didn't seem fair!

That was when I realized how short life is. You don't go through life thinking that your best friend is going to take her life or that you will be at your friend's funeral at the age of 27! We don't think about these things, especially from my background. My mother was always afraid of death. I never could understand why. I knew that when we get old, that was when we would pass on. So, growing up, we never really talked about it. Maybe that could be why Sabrina's death hit me like a ton of bricks. Not only was I hurting because I just lost someone so close to me, but I was struggling to understand because no one ever told me that something like this could happen. No one ever warned me about this stuff! Why would they? Unfortunately, mental illness and suicide are still taboo, and everyone is so afraid to talk about it. So, of course, all I could ask myself was why? This kind of stuff doesn't happen in my world. It was as if I was stepping into unfamiliar territory.

Since reaching out to Sabrina's family, I was able to find out the details of her funeral. That was when reality was sinking in even more. This was going to be my time to say my final goodbyes. The funeral was set to be the following month. So, I continued living my life because that was all I knew what to do. I had my daughter, Genevieve that needed her mother and a wonderful husband that needed his wife. I tried so hard to keep it all together for them. There was also this growing baby inside of me that needed me the most! However, questions and guilt still rolled in my mind. I worried about Sabrina's children, and I hurt for those girls, and I couldn't help but think about my girls and what their life would be like without me. My anger with Sabrina comes back. Those girls were the light of her life! Why? Why? Why! The whole month of March, I walked with a huge hole in my heart. It was a miracle I was somehow able to be a mother to my girls. Somehow.

April rolls in and Daniel and I were in the middle of buying and selling our home. Which, I highly do not recommend when you're eight months pregnant! Never again! I was also recently at my mother's best friends funeral. Strangely enough, her friend passed away in the hospital on the same day as

Sabrina's passing. I hurt for my mother when she told me. Although she was much older, it still wasn't fair, and she was still too young. The circumstance didn't make sense to me. I felt as if God was trying to show me something, but I couldn't put my head around it just yet. My emotions were all over the place that month as Daniel, and I sold our home and had to temporarily move into his parents while we search for our new home. Again, don't move when you're about to give birth!

It was a week before the funeral, and I am nervous. For multiple reasons really, will there be an open or closed casket? Will I be able to handle that knowing that she's in there? The image of walking up to her coffin played in my head over and over. I start to feel anxious. I'm not ready to say goodbye. All of this was a nightmare, and I was ready to start waking up.

Nothing ever fits you when you're eight months pregnant and it's not socially acceptable wearing sweatpants to a funeral. Although, I'm sure Sabrina would have allowed it! My anxiety turns into freaking out about what to wear. But I know where all my feelings are coming from. Daniel looked at me and said he would go with me to find something to wear. That's comforting from him since he hated shopping but knew I needed him and I couldn't go down this road alone.

I'm wobbling through Target like a lost cat! Why are maternity clothes so hideous? I've walked around the whole maternity section for about 20 minutes.

"I can't do this, I don't want to say goodbye. We are too young; we are too young for this Sabrina!"

After Daniel was able to find something for himself, he comes to the women's section finding me freaking out. Daniel always had a way of keeping me calm. He walked over to me and told me that he would find something for me. A weight has lifted, and he ended up finding something cute and comfy for my super pregnant body! How does one get ready for your best friend's funeral? You don't! None of this is healthy. You don't plan for this! My heart hurts, and all I wanted was my best friend back.

April 9th, 2016, It's the morning of the funeral and, everything in me feels heavy, including my 5-pound belly! Before we leave for the church, my mother in law Karen hugs me and reminds me that I will get through this. Daniel and I leave for the funeral. It looked like it was about to rain, which was perfect because Sabrina loved this type of weather. After a short drive, Daniel parks the car, and I take a deep breath and walk up to the church with my head down. I am holding onto Daniel, and I look up to see Sabrina's aunt, Jacqueline, her mother Rosie, and sister Angie. I instantly gave them a big huge hug. Have you ever hugged someone that shared your pain? It was as if I could feel and hear their broken heart and I held onto that hug just a little longer. It's so painfully hard when you have to walk through darkness alone and what I loved about Sabrina's family was how they made sure I was never alone.

We begin to walk into the church. My heart sinks, even more, when I remember that we are in the same room where she and her husband got married. We were in the same place where I heard her say I do and now this will be the place where I say goodbye. I reach over to the table on my left that has a box of tissues and grab a handful. I look up to the altar, and there was her urn surrounded by many beautiful photos. A part of me was relieved that there was no casket because I don't know if I can handle watching her be buried. Daniel and I sit towards the back because I was afraid to be so close to her urn.

Everyone takes a seat, and the ceremony begins, and of course, as Sabrina would have liked it, It started raining. The music starts playing, and my tears start rolling. As I watch her family go up to the podium and say a few words, I think of what they must be going through. This loss is hurting me tremendously but losing your daughter? They have been in my prayers every since especially for her mother, Rosie. As a mother myself, no mother should have to see their baby go before them.

As the ceremony comes to an end, everyone

goes up to the front to say their goodbyes. Holding onto my ball of tissues, I ask Daniel to wait until we are the last few. I just wasn't ready to say goodbye, which is why I tried to stall, but I know that is how everyone felt as well. Our turn comes up, and Daniel holds onto my right arm as we walk up to her urn, I placed my hand on her urn and whispered, "We are too young to say goodbye like this!"

Everyone was starting to pack up as I was standing there. So, we turn around to walk out of the room, my knees begin to lose feeling, and if it weren't for Daniel holding onto me, I would have fallen to the floor. I just said goodbye to my best friend who was only 26! That was when I realized that this was not a nightmare and I will no longer get to see her, hug her, laugh with her, or celebrate other milestones. She's gone, and I will never get to hear her voice again. It's crazy; I never realized how much you could miss someone's voice until it's gone forever. The warmth I feel when I get to watch home videos and hear her voice again brings so much joy to my heart.

We didn't stay at the reception for very long, but it wasn't because I didn't want to be around Sabrina's family. Even today, I still try to be present in their lives. Having her family in my life makes me feel that I still have a little piece of her in my life. As we were planning on leaving, I made sure to greet Sabrina's grandmother, Chela. She was always so welcoming when we first met. Whenever I look at her, I instantly see Sabrina and her sass! She was sitting next to the television that was playing a slideshow of Sabrina's old photos. I grab her attention and hug her. She apologized that she wasn't able to send me the news sooner, but she did not have any way of getting a hold of me. I told her it was just fine and I am glad that I was able to be here. I've always loved how she treated me like her own. That was just her personality, and if you ever want her opinion, she will give it to you straight! We end our conversation, and I proceed to say my goodbyes to everyone including Sabrina's husband, Matt. That man loved her, and I know without a doubt, his daughters will be taken care of. Daniel and I come home to our sweet Genevieve, and I give her a huge embrace because I can't imagine a life without her. That day, I learned how short life is and how from that moment on, I will learn to be present.

After the funeral, some people may have thought that I got the closure I needed and I was able to move forward. See, the thing is, grieving takes much longer than that and saying your final goodbye was just the beginning of the healing journey. My heart was still bleeding; I will always want my friend back. What the funeral did for me was reminded me that all of this was real life and I wasn't going to wake up from this nightmare. Losing Sabrina to this tragedy was just the beginning to something much bigger. She will forever be in my heart, and I know that she is guiding me through healing. It's because of her whom I thank for saving me and for teaching me the power of empathy and love!

The Beginning Of My Relationship With Sabrina

High School is such an awkward time in all of our lives. I just wanted to fit in with the cool kids. I'll never forget the skater kids that would hang out under the stairs. That was the group I wanted to get to know but never really had the chance. None of them liked me, but I certainly liked some of the boys in that group! So, instead, I made friends with the rest of the crowd! The clique in high school never goes away. I wanted to fit in with the extreme sports kids. So, I dressed in really baggy clothes and tight jeans. I don't know why I ever bothered really! I looked nothing like the girls that they would use to date.

Because I made friends with the rest of the

crowd that meant that I made friends with people in all types of cliques, there was the Goths, the skaters, the rebels, the book nerds, the class clowns, and even the Mormons. You name it; I probably knew at least one person in that group! Where did I ever fit in? I don't know because looking back; I tried so hard to be someone so, I showed people the person they wanted me to be. But, no matter how much I tried, my real friends were the ones that saw who the real Diana was. Those were the friends that have helped me grow into the woman I am today!

Now, not all of these friends are still in my life, but I genuinely believe that some people come into your life for a season and others for a lifetime. We are continually growing, and we all have different journeys but I've always meant well for whomever I was able to cross paths with.

Sabrina was one of the rebels and she was also gorgeous. So of course, she instantly intimidated me. After years of crossing paths and just having mutual friends, Sabrina and I became friends. I can't remember who introduced us but it was during our senior year, and we had three other mutual friends. There was Jackie whom I've known for years, and we both shared the same first jobs! Then we had Rachel, the bookworm compared to all of us! Even though I may not have seen it back then, her smarts and compassion truly inspired me! After ten years, she still holds a similar personality. There was also Robin! She was also Filipino and grew up in a strict home, and that was how we bonded. It's not easy having foreign parents in American culture. She was usually someone I turned to for advice when my parents were not hearing me.

Finally, after four years of high school, I found

my clique! A small group of gals that loved me for the person that I was and able to just be me! I still very much love these girls, and although we may not see each other as much as we used to, we are all still able to keep each other up with everything through social media!

Sabrina and I were finally getting to know each other better as we were lucky enough to share the same lunch period! Once I was able to see the real her, I noticed something. She was shy, but she also puts up a wall. During our last year in high school, I wasn't able to pinpoint what she was hiding. There was a girl in there hurting, but she felt that everyone had to see someone strong and brave!

Why are we so afraid of showing others our pain? We all have brokenness. This world is not perfect, but we all seem to be good at acting like it is!

Something that I've learned about being broken is that it only makes us stronger! Not to say that we heal and bury our hurt. I want others to see my scars. I feel empowered when I can share my story and how I've survived. I faced pain, and I'm sure that wouldn't be the last of it! As the storm comes and goes, I pick up each broken pieces and start over until I get something right.

It was a whole two years after our graduation until Sabrina, Jackie and I saw each other again. Everyone else kind of just started their own lives. Rightfully so, high school was finally over, and it was our time to shine. A part of my separation was my fault. All I wanted was to find my identity and move out on my own so; I did everything I could to get there. I landed a decent job, paid my car off, and was saving money for my first apartment. Of course, all in the mix of that, I fcll in love with this sweet innocent Italian boy. That was a season in my life where I learned to fall in love and fall out of love. I got caught up with trying to figure out my own life experience that I pretty much left high school behind. As I am sitting here typing this, I wish I hadn't left my friends behind. Maybe I would have been gifted with more time with Sabrina before she left this place we call earth.

In 2009, two years after our graduation, Jackie contacted me and told me that she was going to be in town for Christmas! She had moved to Colorado after high school so that she too can find her identity. I was so excited to see her again and meet my then fiancé....who was not Daniel! Yes, I was engaged twice! I told ya'll this was a season where I also learned how I fell out of love for the first time. Once Jackie came to town, we had all planned to meet up at one of the big casinos here in Las Vegas. She also brought

30

Sabrina with her, and I was happy to see her again too. It was like a mini reunion!

After our little get together, I realized that I was living a life that wasn't the true me. I felt trapped in this world that I created for myself. A world that I thought I wanted. You see, I was afraid to be alone, which is why I first got engaged at a young age of 20. The truth is, I wasn't ready to get married. What I wanted was to be able to explore, and my fiancé was holding me back from doing just that. I remembered looking over and Jackie and Sabrina thinking about how they are free to fly. That is what I wanted! I wanted to know what it was like to be free and not have to answer to anyone else but my own. Little did I know that all of my other friends were trying to figure out their identity as well. Little did I know that Sabrina must have been feeling that same way! Oh, how I had no idea that my sweet friend Sabrina didn't see how beautiful she was.

It was later that year in 2010 when I decided I needed to remove that engagement ring on my left finger and decided to start a life of my own. Hours were spent searching on craigslist for a roommate. Call after call, and my palms would sweat in fear after I've made that call.

"Hello, my name is Diana, and I am wondering if you still have that room available?"

Not only was I so afraid of starting this new life but I was also hurting. I intended never to hurt my ex-fiancé's heart. I prayed for him to find love better than me and I still say that prayer for him. He did nothing wrong, and he was oh so very loyal, but it was all me.

Something in my heart was still missing, and I decided to search for that missing piece of my life.

I always told others that Sabrina and I were friends since high school, but we didn't bond until after our 21st birthday. I'll always wish she could have given me more time with her here on earth but I will forever be grateful for the years she has given me. 2010 was also the year where we were all old enough to drink! So, the bars and clubs were where we were. I tried my hand at playing with the slot machines but I never really had quite the patience for such thing. There was a night when Jackie and I were playing at a nearby local casino, and I am getting angry because I just lost a few dollars while Jackie is to my right winning a few bucks! That was when I gave up on the whole gambling thing! It was a big year for all of us! That was the year I met Daniel and Sabrina finally met her husband. When Sabrina told me about her new man when we were sitting at the bar, I felt that was when we started bonding as friends. Sabrina was the gal who would keep everything inside especially the dark days. Which is why it hurt so much when she has passed because although she had shown me a little of her darkness, even I didn't see her whole broken heart. Had I known her pain, would I have been able to save her? It's a question I ask myself all the time!

It was a year later when she was planning a trip to upstate New York to meet her man's family. A little piece of me knew she would have come home with a ring of her finger! Come on, meeting the parents is indeed a big deal! I waited a whole month before I decided that it was time for Daniel to meet my family. It wasn't because I was afraid they wouldn't like him; I was more fearful of Daniel running away from my crazy family! Good thing he stuck around! Sometimes Asian families can be too much to handle!

It was after Sabrina's trip when we found out that she was getting married! I was so excited for her, but there was also a little part of me hoping that maybe Daniel would propose next. Envy and comparison is such a mood killer for us girls. I did that a lot when it came to Sabrina. It wasn't that I didn't like her. She was a fantastic friend, but I certainly envied her beauty. During that time in my life, I felt like I was on some race! Who was going to get married first? Who would be successful first? It was exhausting trying to keep up with everyone, but I felt that I had to prove myself to everyone! Once I was able to find my true identity just this past year, I learned that this feeling of being like everyone or being better then everyone came from my childhood. When I was growing up, no one ever told me that I was good at something. Instead, I was told what I should be doing to be successful. Have I mentioned that everyone in my family wanted me to be a nurse? Well, I indeed was a disappointment!

After Sabrina's death, I slowly became closer to her family and especially Grandma Chela. I've always loved her for her open kindness and sassiness! She is very much like Sabrina. I've come to grow comfortable with Grandma Chela, and I would spend hours at her house just chatting. She's a very inspirational woman! I'll never forget one visit; She was telling me more about Sabrina and some things she may have hidden from her friends. You see, the Sabrina I knew was strong and powerful, but according to Grandma Chela, there was another Sabrina that hid from everyone else. She told me how Sabrina struggled with her appearance and didn't feel as beautiful as others portray her to be. My heart sank after hearing the truth. Here I was comparing myself to Sabrina and being jealous of her beauty, and deep down, Sabrina was hurting and felt that she was anything but beautiful. In all the years of knowing this sweet person, I never knew how much pain she carried in her heart. After she left us, I always made sure to tell her how I wished she had told me. Maybe I could have saved her; perhaps I could have been that one friend that would have made a difference. It's far too late to know the answers now, but I know that she knows this now.

I look back ten years ago and remember that young teenager Diana that first met Sabrina and think about what I first thought about her. To me, she was strong and a loyal friend. She had her troubles when we were teens, but I figured that was because we were annoying teenagers! Little did I know that she was hurting on the inside. That was when I learned to never judge a book by its cover. She has taught me the power of empathy and how although someone may look "perfect" on the outside, it could be a total mess inside. I hope she knows how much everyone would have still loved her no matter the scars and hurt she carried. You don't always have to be strong for everyone. Being vulnerable and sharing this story to others is not easy. I could easily bury my pain, but that doesn't do me any good. I wasn't able to help Sabrina, but she has given me that strength to help someone else.

We aren't in High School Anymore

It was a cold Christmas of 2011 and Daniel, and I was driving to his parent's house for their Christmas get together. Although we were not living together at the time, Daniel was practically at my place all the time. We were dating for a year and a half had fallen in love fairly quickly. I've always been someone who would wear my heart of my sleeve, but with Daniel it was different. I knew there was something special with him and I made sure not to mess it up. So, I took my time and enjoyed our growing relationship. During our short drive back to his parent's I joked and asked Daniel if he was going to propose next Christmas. He looked at me and said, "Well, why do I have to wait a whole year?" Honestly, I was shocked and excited! So excited that I went to buy my wedding dress a month before he even proposed! No seriously, I was that excited! The best part was that it took Daniel a few years later to realize the truth about the dress! Because the date of when I bought the dress and the day he actually proposed was so close, he naturally thought I bought it after the proposal. I guess it was a good thing he was actually serious about marrying me!

It was February 2012, and I had just come back from a seminar. The housing market was so crazy at the time, and my roommate recommended that I should buy my first house. No, it wasn't because she was trying to get rid of me! It was just a great opportunity and investment. So, I agreed and started the process of becoming a first-time homebuyer! Before meeting with Daniel that weekend, I was at a seminar where they would teach you all the things about being a first-time homebuyer. Before I left, I received a text from Daniel that he wasn't going to be at my house that afternoon because his parent needed help with some computer issues. He had his own key to my place, and we planned on spending the evening together. So, I went home and waited for him to come over. Once he was finally done, he recommended that we go out to a fancy dinner.

I asked where we should go, and he suggested we go to "Kona Grill" which just so happens to be the same restaurant where we had our first date! I didn't think anything of it but was excited to have some delicious food! Have I ever told you that food makes me a very happy person? Yup! After I tell Daniel all about my seminar and how excited I am to get this house, we left for our date. At that time, the jobbing market was not so great, and Daniel had to move back into his parents, so, naturally, he was going to move into my new place with me. Initially, the plan was to move in together before marriage! Yes, that did not make my parents all that excited! They were very old school and the fact that I was an unmarried woman living on my own and having a man spending the night with me was forbidden! I never followed the rules, and I wasn't going to change now! Little did I know that my plan was going to change just a little bit!

We finally make it to Kona Grill and of course, I ask for a mojito! There I was in the semi-dark restaurant looking at Daniel. I am getting a little buzzed, but I did remember him telling me about how weddings were performed in ancient Rome. He's a total history nerd! He then holds my hand and instantly gets on one knee. I can see that he was so nervous, like, the man was shaking nervous, but of course, I said yes! Now, I don't know if you know this or it's the same for every Asian, but when I drink even just a little, my face will turn completely red! So, the waiter happened to see Daniel propose and she offered to take a photo and brought champagne! I thought, a picture? For everyone to see how drunk I am right now! Well, it's now or never, and this time around, I was planning NOT to get engaged again! So, once we announced our engagement to everyone, that exact photo was shared. I did not look pretty what so ever and if I could maybe redo that day, I totally would!

On October 26th of 2012, I became Diana Collins, and my new husband carried me into our first home! So many memories were made in that little two-story home. Our wedding day was perfect with just enough friends and family. I come from a huge family, but I made it clear that I didn't want anything significant. There were less than 100 guests, and we all had a great time. However, I'll never forget how much Daniel hated dancing! He was sweet for trying, but half of my family is Filipino; you better believe the majority was on that dance floor! It was a perfect day.

I looked for Sabrina that day because she told me the day before that she would be attending. Of course, it hurt my feelings. I was there for her on her special day, and she couldn't have given me just one day? That night, I tried to bury my feelings because I wasn't going to let it ruin my wedding day of course. As soon as everything was settled, I soon received a message from Sabrina saying that she thought it was the day after. Of course, the usual me accepted her apology but did not really talk about my feelings. I was afraid to explain my feelings to her because I didn't want to seem selfish or start an argument.

I buried my feelings so deep that that was the

same year when Sabrina and I cut ties and ended our friendship. This is something I still regret today because it was mostly my fault. I didn't know how to express my feelings to her. So instead, I just distanced myself. Sabrina found out that she was expecting her first child around the same time as my wedding day. Which was why she got her day confused because she was dealing with her own emotions. Now that I am a mother of two, this explanation made complete sense to me, but when I was just a newlywed, I had no idea what she was talking about and felt that she was trying to look for an excuse.

We were all growing up into adulthood, and I felt that our lives were going into two different directions. When Daniel and I first got married, we had agreed to start having children five years after being married. So, because Sabrina was expecting her first child and I wouldn't get pregnant for another five years, I was not able to resonate with her life changes. A real friend would be in her life even if they were in different seasons of life. Unfortunately, that was difficult for me, and that made me feel like a terrible friend. I should have been there for her either way. She was probably terrified and needed her friend's support. Because I let my envy get the best of me that was when I decided to end our friendship. She even asked why and I couldn't give her an answer. How could I have told her that I was jealous of her and her "perfect" life? How can I tell her that I was ready to have a child and hurting because my husband was not yet prepared? Little did I know that had I told her all of these things, she would have been right there to support me because she was that type of friend. I was afraid of being judged just like how I've always been when we were in high school. Problem is, we are no longer in high school, and I was having a hard time letting go of that mindset.

I lost a year of what could have been a beautiful friendship with Sabrina. I practically missed her whole pregnancy and the birth of her sweet baby girl. It was precisely one year after the breakup when I found out that I was expecting my first! I was over the moon excited, and unfortunately, I didn't even think Sabrina would find out or even care. But, I was wrong, and she proves her loyalty once again. It was the spring of 2014 and Sabrina's firstborn was about to have her first birthday. I hopped onto my computer one night to work on some schoolwork and found that I had a message on Facebook from her. I was very nervous even to open the email. I slowly drag my mouse over to the message and click open.

She said that she found out that I was expecting through our mutual friend Jackie and she wanted to congratulate me. My heart instantly just sank. I missed our friendship and was sad because no one in my friend circle was expecting. Somehow she knew I needed her support as I walk into motherhood. We got to talk and eventually agreed to meet up somewhere and chat. Oh great, now I have to look at her in the face and tell her I was just envious of her? I was so embarrassed I even felt that way towards her.

It was one evening after work, and we had agreed to meet at a Starbucks that was near her grandmother, Chela's house. I walked into the coffee shop and ordered myself an iced coffee and sat down. Reaching out for my phone, I sent her a text that I was there. No response, so I waited and thought maybe she was on the way and couldn't answer. It was thirty minutes after the time we were supposed to meet up, and she never showed. I left angry and disappointed. This was a part of the reason why I couldn't be her friend anymore. In my mind, she was a flake, and I wanted so much for her to be in my life, but I couldn't handle any more of these disappointments. I hurry home to Daniel in tears and found comfort in his arms for the rest of the night.

The next day, I get a text from Sabrina apologizing for not showing up. She said that she was very ill that day and wasn't able to get out of the house. Of course, I had my doubts on whether the story was true or not but I forgave her and told her that we will have to try again soon. Keeping my guard up, we made plans to meet again. I didn't want to get hurt again so; naturally, I expected her not to show up. That was something I would usually do when I was waiting for something to happen. I always thought that if I would just predict that the negative would happen, I wouldn't get hurt! So, that is what I did. I got to our meeting place and told her I would be at the frozen yogurt shop. To my surprise, she showed up! It was so lovely to see her again, and although I always felt that Sabrina was a flake, she always came to you with open arms and a loving heart. That was something I loved most about her.

After the small talk, it didn't take us long to start talking about what happened to our friendship. From what I can remember, I believe that Sabrina was the one that pushed the conversation into that direction. Oh, there goes my stomach in knots again. If I told her the truth about how I felt, she would either be angry or think I was crazy. I couldn't tell her that a part of why I had to keep my distance was because I was jealous! It was so silly of me to feel that way in the first place. So, I ended up only telling her half of the truth, which was that I thought that our lives were going into separate directions and that we were not spending time together as much as we used to. I felt that I was being left out into her new life. That was the truth; I just left out the little detail of comparing my self worth to hers! The conversation ended with grace, and she ended up inviting me to her daughters first birthday! I told her I wouldn't miss it! At that time I was just 8 weeks pregnant, and the sickness only recently subsided so, I was really looking forward to having real food again! Sabrina's family parties were always the best!

Our friendship had been reborn but in a different season, a season of motherhood! This was where we really started to bond. I may not have known this at the time but God knew we needed each other and I will always be so grateful for the last two years

of her beautiful friendship she had gifted me.

So, This is Motherhood

Sabrina and I would always try our best to have play dates or just simply spend time with one another but between my work schedule, her being a mom, and both of us having all of our families in town, life just always seemed to get in our way. Now that I know she was struggling with depression, I understood why she really did not want to come out and socialize. Depression can literally suck the life out of you. There were so many times where I would create an argument in my own mind debating if I should go to that play date or dinner party. By the time I had my children dressed, I was ready to get back into bed and fall asleep. Most of the time, Sabrina and I would socialize via text message or behind a computer screen. So, although we may not have seen each other regularly, we always were supporting each other any way that we could! There was one evening where I was about four months pregnant with Genevieve, and I get a text message from her telling me that she will not be able to donate her baby items to me. At first, I was taken back by that statement but she quickly explained that she was going to still need them in nine months! We were both so excited to be pregnant around the same time, and I was even more honored to know that I was one of the firsts of many to hear about the wonderful news! It was the first time I would get to share this pregnancy journey with one of my best friends. Although she was a whole trimester behind me, I was going to enjoy this moment!

It was Christmas Day 2014 was when I noticed I was having some persistent contractions. These contractions have been coming and going for the whole third trimester. That was when I learned how much I hated Braxton hicks! Is it time? Did I time my contractions? Oh, the anxiety and excitement filled the whole family! Everyone knew that Genevieve was to make her appearance the next day, but I had a feeling she would either come on Christmas day or a week late. We were celebrating Christmas at Daniel's parents house, and I was sitting next to his grandmother, Betty. Bless her soul; I just adored her so much. Every time a contraction would come through, I was let out a very loud grunt! The family didn't know to either pack my bags or laugh at me! Grandma Betty however smiled and coached me through them. It was a Christmas that could never be forgotten.

Daniel and I ended up heading home later that evening because I just needed to lie down in bed. I was getting used to these Braxton hicks and would think nothing us them unless they were really close in time. It was past midnight, December 26th, 2014; I had a contraction strong enough to wake me up. My doctor told me that when I had these Braxton hicks, I should try to use the bathroom. So, that is exactly what I did. I walked into the bathroom, sat on the toilet and just like that, my water broke!

Being that I had no idea what I was supposed to do, I yelled for Daniel and stood in the shower while my water continued to flow! It was the funniest thing I've ever seen! Daniel hurried and called labor and delivery to ask what our next steps would be, and we packed our stuff and went to the hospital to have a baby! Of course, I didn't have time to tell everyone, and they were all most likely asleep, so I waited for a decent hour to let the family and my closet friends know I was in labor.

The contractions surprisingly didn't make me lose my mind like everyone else thought would happen. I am not one to tolerate pain very well, but I always remembered my breathing. I thought that if I can put my mind on that, I wouldn't notice the pain! However, once I got to 3cm, I was already asking for the epidural! After 16 hours of labor, I didn't progress fast enough, and the baby's heart rate kept going down, as she would descend past the birth canal. "The cord could possibly be wrapped around her neck." is what my nurse would tell me and I freaked a little, but I trusted the doctor's decision to go ahead and get C-section. (Caesarean section)

My mother was coming back from the vending machines, while they wheeled me into the OR and she was instantly in tears. Of course, a mother would be worried about her daughter having to go into surgery but it was nice to know that she was concerned as it was at that time when I needed my mother. There hadn't been many times when I thought I would need her, but at that moment, where I was about to become a mother myself, that was when I needed her the most. "It's going to be ok Diana. Just pray. Just pray." She said to me as I was being wheeled away.

As I lay on that table wanting to literally puke, I hear my little girl's sweet cry! Within minutes, Daniel and I were parents! Although I was not able to hold my daughter right after, Daniel brought her over to me, and I gave her a kiss. Nothing else mattered at that moment, we were a family of three, and I became a mother! Let the journey of motherhood begin!

Healing from a C-section was not what I had planned and was still really shocked about what happened. There I was trying to recover from what happened, but I must say, I was not the best patient to have. I couldn't understand what was going on with my body. Why was everything swollen? Why is the epidural making me so itchy? I know I took a birthing class at that very hospital and I don't remember anyone preparing me for this. I felt that I wasn't prepared for motherhood at all. You expect me to take care of this tiny human on my own?

My doctor finally released me about four days after Genevieve was born and I couldn't have been happier. Both Daniel and I hated being in the hospital, even though I worked at one for almost a decade, being the patient was never my favorite. I was nervous, I felt like my body failed me. What kind of woman was I if I wasn't able to give birth the natural way? Wasn't this what I was made for?

The ride home was very short as it was just down the street. It was the coldest day in winter, and I was more than excited that we didn't have a long drive home. We were all exhausted, and I was still in some severe pain. Daniel's parents helped us out of the hospital and told us they were going to pick up dinner while we drove back home. It honestly does take a village to raise a family and although I may not have realized how blessed I was, to have my whole family there with me was a special gift.

Motherhood became a reality once everyone had left and It was just the three of us. "Can I handle this? Am I even fit to be a mother?" I was still shocked about the C-section. I just never thought this would happen to me. Everything I've ever read made labor and delivery look like it was going to rain glitter and I would instantly feel joy! What I really felt was fear and physical pain!

Daniel was able to take a total of two weeks off to help me heal and take me to my follow up appointments but once those two weeks quickly came to an end, It was just Genevieve and I. Here came the fear and anxiety again. They called it the fourth trimester and boy was it the hardest trimester. I was alone with a newborn baby! My brain became mush and taking care of myself was the last priority. There was one time where I even tried to make a meal in the microwave and almost burnt the house down! I guess instead of putting one-minute cook time, I put ten and didn't even think twice. It took a village, but I was afraid to ask for help. I didn't want to be a burden to anyone. This is what society told me, I was supposed to know how to do all of this! Right?

Although it was a rough 12 weeks, I had an

excellent time bonding with my sweet daughter. The week before I was supposed to go back to work was a very emotional one for me. That was when I knew I wanted to find a way to work from home or have a more flexible schedule. I became envious of all the stay at home moms that didn't have to leave their baby behind. My first day back to work was a total mess. I couldn't stop thinking about Genevieve and what she was doing or if she was sleeping on her schedule. You know, everything the "books" told me to do! Slowly, I've learned to calm down a bit, but it was not a smooth transition. I enjoyed working at the hospital, but I knew that if I wanted to become the mother I wanted to be, this kind of work schedule would not make that happen.

Three months after coming back to work, I decided to make a career shift. I've worked at the same hospital for seven years, but I was also in school to become a teacher. Yes, that is correct, not only was I a new working mom, I was in school still trying to get my degree! I slowly learned that it was not the right path to my future.

April of 2015, I accepted my first teaching position at a local daycare. This is what I thought I needed and thought would help me become the mother I wanted to be. Soon after accepting the job, I quickly learned that this was not my destiny. I was not becoming the mother I wanted, in fact, I was away from my family more often than before. Turns out the grass weren't greener on the other side. If I wasn't meant to be a teacher than what was I expected to do with my life? What am I suppose to be when I grow up?

Life as a working mother and student became

overwhelming. I was failing in school and felt like I was failing at life. That was when depression was starting to make its appearance. However, because I wasn't educated on the topic, I didn't think anything of it. I just assumed that I was stressed and hoped it would all end in time.

Is this what motherhood was supposed to feel like? I felt as if I was just surviving and not enjoying the world around me. I couldn't just quit my job. Now that I am a mother, I couldn't just jump and make crazy life decisions. But I was tired and just wanted more time with my family.

What is the Key to Success?

It's Sunday night, and we are all upset because we don't want the weekend to end. We dread the 40-hour work week, and the term Monday blues is used regularly. I have been working since I was 16 years old and I've always dreaded having to go into work, especially a job that wasn't making me happy. My father used to tell me that I should just be thankful I had a job and focus on working for the paycheck. But I always wanted to ask him, why? What is the point of life if you're going to be miserable living it? Didn't God put us here to live out our life's purpose? I'm sure he wouldn't want to see us wasting away our gift of life! All I wanted was to find a way to be happy and pay my bills while doing it.

Soon after graduating from high school, my parents

wanted to know what I wanted to do with my life. To be honest, I was looking forward to getting away from my parents and live a life I've been dreaming of for years. That was a life of freedom and being able to make my own decisions! The last thing on my mind was college or having a career. But, my parents told me otherwise, and I had to get a job and attend college. I know they only want what was best for me, but they never accepted the person that I was on the inside. I was a creator, but creators don't make money, and I had to leave that worthless dream behind.

After the summer of 2007, my father recommends a desk job opening that I should apply for. That was my first "real" job that I ended up staying in for seven years until I became a mother myself. They wanted me to become a nurse because that was the only way to live a successful life. However, after working in a hospital for years, I've seen how run down these doctors and nurse were. Was that the life I wanted to live? Working day and night, 12-hour shifts, patients yelling at you for more pain meds, and so much more! Now, don't get me wrong, I think these people are lovely people that are saving lives but that wasn't the life I ever pictured myself having.

Whenever someone would ask me what I wanted to be when I grow up, I would come up with so many things because when you are the age of 6 and older, do you ever really know? I told my teachers I wanted to be a singer, an artist, a graphic designer, or even a fashion designer! Everything that was listed had to do with using my creative side of my brain. But, no one ever gave me the tools to pursue those dreams. My family would tell me, "You'll never make any money doing that Diana!" "Do you see how much these nurses are making? Isn't that what you want? A life without worry?"

Does having lots of money really bring you happiness? Can you actually buy happiness? I had spent so many nights crying myself to sleep because I wasn't allowed to do what my heart desired. My twenties were flying by, and I was still attending college with no real focus on every completing a degree. I had no real direction, and everyone just looked at me as though I was some lost sheep! I thought to myself, "I can't keep doing this, there has got to be a better life out there somewhere."

After being in school for what seemed like forever, I was 23 and getting ready to become, Mrs. Diana Collins! At that point in my life, work was just something I did to pay my mortgage. I would clock in, complete my daily tasks and clock out. With still having the mindset of having to complete a college degree to be happy, I was still taking some college classes here and there. Mostly just to make my parents and everyone else happy. I've changed my major many times, so much that I've had the school counselor comment with how incompetent I was! "I see you've changed majors multiple times. Hmm." That was exactly what he said to me. Way to motivate someone I thought to myself.

Eventually, I went into early childhood education and loved it! So much that after having my first-born Genevieve, I decided to leave my hospital job and pursue a career in teaching. After much searching, I accepted a position as a preschool teacher. It was only after a few months when I realized that this wasn't what I wanted and it just made me miss my daughter that much more!

I was getting tired of myself! "I can't have my cake and eat it too!" That is what my father would always tell me, and it would annoy me more and more. Why not? Why couldn't I live a life of complete happiness? True happiness was what I had at home with my little family but if I wasn't happy with my career, how can I come home and be present with my family if I was so miserable! It was like I was running 100 mph and nothing was stopping me! There was no time for self-care for this working mom. There had to be something more to life! Is Motherhood really this hard? Is this what I signed up for? Why didn't anyone tell me it was going to be this hard? The moms in the books, blogs, and magazines seemed like they were doing it just fine. So, why was I having so much trouble?

The summer of 2015 was a very stressful time. I was angry at myself. I hated the job that I thought would bring me joy and I also dropped out of college and was now left in debt! How could I have thought that I could do it all? I felt so stupid for thinking that I can be a working mother and still attempt at getting my college degree. "It takes discipline, Diana! All you need is to focus!" How the hell could I focus on something that I hated? Attending school was never meant for me, and I was being pushed away from what I really wanted to do! I just wanted a career where I can have the freedom to create something!

Towards the end of summer, the stress got to me so much that I didn't even notice that my period was weeks late! I had my suspicions, but I wasn't really showing any symptoms. Genevieve was only nine months old when I found out that I was pregnant with her baby sister, Teresa. A working mother with two under two? How on earth was I going to be able to do this? I'm already having trouble being a mom with one! Teresa was a blessing to our family, but it was me that I was worried about. I felt that my children deserve someone that had her stuff together. What kind of mother will I be if I was always a complete hot mess?!

Working at the preschool was getting harder as I got bigger and was experiencing constant colds due to the nature of the job! I was six months along and couldn't take it anymore. My back was killing me, and my emotions were all over the place. The amount of stress was getting to me and wasn't safe for my unborn child. One day during my lunch break. I ran into the bathroom and called Daniel in a panic. I told him that couldn't take this anymore and we had to figure something out to help me. Soon after that conversation, he found out that there was a position at his office and I was more than welcome to apply for!

I gave up my career of working as a teacher, and administrative work was all that I knew! So, I took the job and started right away! Working with Daniel and being able to carpool with him did make things a little easier. I began accepting the fact that I was a college drop out and gave up trying to earn that college degree. It didn't matter to me, and all I wanted was to be a present mom for my children. Daniel knew how much I wanted this so he continued to work harder so that we can find a way to afford to have me stay at home with the kids.

After only working at the office for just one month, I found out about Sabrina's passing, and that was when my whole world crashed. I felt like I was already hanging by the wire and finding of this tragedy was what sent me to rock bottom. Being that I was in constant pain, my work ethic started to suffer. I couldn't focus for months, and all I could do was sit in the corner of my cubicle and cry! The office was about 90% male, and whenever someone did catch me crying at my desk, no one really knew what they could do for me. Not even my own husband was able to help me. I was drowning and drifting away from reality more and more every single day.

"Why can't I get my shit together?"

"Why is Sabrina not here to comfort me?"

"Life makes no sense! How can someone so young no longer be here on earth?"

We are faced with death every day and hear stories about young people losing their lives to violence, illness, and even mental illness but, when it happens in your own backyard, life gives you a whole new meaning. That was when I learned that suicide and depression was actually a real thing and that you never know what someone else can be struggling with.

A New Baby and a Broken Heart

I was due on May 2nd of 2016; I was 40 weeks pregnant with no sign of going into labor! Daniel was planning to go to work that day but I begged him to stay with me as I figured the same would happen with Genevieve and Teresa would easily arrive on her due date. Daniel worked an hour away from home, and although I knew we couldn't afford him taking the day off, I didn't want to go into labor and have him be so far away from us. It was hard for me to explain that the only support I wanted was from him and not anyone else.

He finally agreed to stay, and we go to my final OB appointment together. My birth plan was simple, I wanted to have a VBAC (Vaginal birth after cesarean) and being that I had some issues with my first labor, my doctor and I agreed to go in for an induction the next day. Later that night, we waited on the phone call from the hospital telling us when to come in. The call comes in earlier than expected, and the nurse on the other line asked if we would be able to head over to the hospital around ten o' clock that night. I was already so uncomfortable and ready to give birth that I didn't think twice about the induction! My bags were packed over a week ago, and all we had to do was to say goodbye to our sweet Genevieve. This was very hard for me to do and I was dreading it for months. This would be the first night and a few days after that where we would not be able to kiss her goodnight, and it broke my heart just a little bit. At the time, we were temporarily living with Daniel's parents while we look for our new home and so that made things pretty simple for us. Before we left for the hospital, we gathered together to say a prayer and off we went to have another beautiful baby!

Although it took a little to get over the shock of having two little ones at the same time, I was over the moon excited to meet Teresa and watch her grow with Genevieve! I knew they would instantly make the best of friends and believed in the Lord's plan for us. However, that joy of becoming a mother again was soon overtaken by the pain of missing my best friend, Sabrina. I felt so broken and sad that she wouldn't be coming over to the hospital to visit Teresa and me! My attitude soon shifted that night, and I went from joy to just wanting to get it over with so that I can get back home with my family. I tried to have faith in God that night, but it was hard when I was so angry that my friend was no longer here. All I wanted was her to be here and tell me that everything was going to be ok!

Once I got settled in my labor and delivery room, my nurse came in to talk about the plan. I told her about my desire to have a VBAC, but I understood that there is no guarantee and I was mentally prepared for a C-section if that was my only option. She informed me that because I was post-surgery in less than 2 years, I had a risk of tearing my scar open. Yes, that sounds awful, and my anxiety would have kicked in full gear at the time, but I was so numb in my emotions of grief that I didn't even connect what my nurse just told me. I looked at her and said, ok, I guess we will just try our best not to let that happen! Because of the risk, my doctor would only allow me to labor no more than eight hours.

No one ever told me that having an induction meant worse contractions! Once I was over my breathing techniques, I called the nurse and told her to get the epidural! To everyone's shock, I've always handled labor reasonably well! I think I just didn't want to scare anyone with my screaming, so I did my best to focus on my breathing, and once I was ready for help, I made sure my nurse knew!

Even with the help of Pitocin, I was pushing the eight-hour mark and stopped dilating. My nurses and doctor all came in to talk about the next step which was to go into the OR and not knowing what else to do, I put my trust in them and agreed for the C-section. Once we were all on the same page, my nurse told everyone that she would call my primary OB/GYN to inform her of the plan. Daniel and I figured it would be a minute before they can prep us to go into the OR, so he went to use the bathroom. It wasn't even five minutes and all of a sudden, I see my nurse running in and quickly unplugging everything! "What's happening!", I said in an anxious tone. "The baby's heart rate is dropping, and we need to rush you in NOW!", She replied. Just as the rest of the medical team was wheeling me away, I yell for Daniel to hurry up and get out of the bathroom! I can't imagine what he felt realizing all of this chaos was going on while he was on the toilet!

My births have always felt like they ended in traumatic situations. The last thing I wanted was to have to heal from this surgery. Although I was mentally prepared, it indeed wasn't my first choice. Will, I ever experience the birth of my dreams? Is having a "magical" birth really a thing or is that something that was made up? I wanted so much to be able to hold my baby the minute she was born, but I was never even given that opportunity!

The moment Teresa was born, Daniel brought

her over to me, and she just took my breath away! She was a little 5 pound 19 oz and looked just like her father! Although I ended up having a crazy birth experience, I was so happy to finally move onto the next chapter in our lives, raising our family or four! After a few days of being in the hospital, Daniel and I were so happy to be going home with our new baby. We also hated being stuck in the hospital, and Daniel's back was dying after sleeping on a couch for 3 days! Hospitals should really do something about that! Dad's need to sleep too you know!

Our lives were a bit hectic when Teresa was born. Since we were still looking for a new home, we did not bring Teresa home in her new home because we were staying at my in-laws. Which was totally fine but when 90 percent of your belongings were locked up in a storage unit, it felt like a part of my life was missing! My stress levels went through the roof! I was dealing with Sabrina's death, buying/selling a home, and giving birth to our second child! I did my best to keep my cool, but with my anxiety and inadequate coping skills, I was toxic to my whole family.

With my life running at 100 mph, I never really spent the time actually to grieve the loss of Sabrina. I was really good at burying my hurt and letting everyone else know that I was perfectly fine! But, I wasn't ok! It was two weeks after Teresa, and I were discharged and the heartache was rushing through my veins. Sabrina was supposed to be here. She was supposed to cheer me on, and our kids were going to be the best of friends! How did this happen? Why did this happen?

One afternoon, those thoughts came rushing through. They were telling me that if Sabrina couldn't handle being a mother of two, what makes me different? I sat there in bed with a newborn baby in my arms thinking, "They are right. How am I capable of raising two young children? I am broken, and it will be my fault if I pass that onto them! I can't do that to them. Everyone is better off without me!" That was when the thought of grabbing my husband's gun came in, and I couldn't stop thinking about it! I wanted the pain to stop! I would have done anything to make them stop!

That was the very first time I've ever considered harming myself, and I was utterly terrified of myself! It was as if a complete stranger took over me and this stranger did not like me very well! I quickly became so afraid for Teresa and I so I grabbed my phone and called the suicide hotline. This was all happening while my in-laws were in the living room taking care of Genevieve. The lady on the other line had a soft, calm voice. Would she even know the pain in my heart? Is she going to call the police and take my children away?

I was afraid to tell her the truth about wanting to take my own life, but eventually, the truth came out, and I figured she would have found out anyways. I told her that I recently lost my best friend and I am not coping well. After just talking for maybe fifteen minutes, she was able to calm my nerves. It was nice telling someone that I wasn't ok. My whole family just expected me to snap out of it and move on. None of them ever really lost someone to such a tragedy, and they just didn't know what else to do. I felt so isolated in my own heartache!

After my phone call with the hotline, I quickly grabbed my insurance card and called for a referral to a therapist. I've been to a therapist before when I was in my early 20s before having kids but I knew that therapist didn't take my insurance and I couldn't afford to pay out of pocket. So, I was hoping I would be sent to someone that could really help me. I made my appointment for the following week, and as I sat there with Teresa, I thought, "It's postpartum depression. They warned me about this! That's ok, I'll get help, and this will all be a thing of the past!" The next eight months had proven to be otherwise and going to a therapist was just the beginning of my healing journey.

The Moment I Hit Rock Bottom

Being a Mother of two and working an hour away from home was getting to be overwhelming. It was months after Sabrina's death, and I still could not keep it together. Postpartum depression was hitting me hard but I never really had time to get help and follow through with treatment. No one around me understood my pain. They said that I should be over her death by now; I had to move on with my life. What they didn't know was that my struggles were far past dealing with death, I was experiencing PTSD (Post-traumatic stress disorder) from my childhood. I didn't realize it at the time but something triggered it all, and that something was the pressure of raising two children at a very young age.

I struggled with self-doubt my whole life. I

was never good enough for anyone; thus when I became a mother, I felt that I wouldn't be good at the job. What was I thinking? I said to myself, "I should have never become a mother!" My house was always a complete mess, every morning my whole family was digging for clothes because the laundry was never done, and I was also failing at work. That was when the negative voices would haunt me.

"Look at you!"

"You suck at this!"

"You suck at life!"

"Your mother was right!"

"Just do it. You know how just take your life."

"Everyone would be better off without you."

Daniel was taking some night classes in the fall and

once a week, I was left alone to put the girls to sleep. It was never easy as none of my children were great sleepers. Once Teresa was born, It completely changed Genevieve's sleep routine and stopped sleeping through the night. Both of the girls needed me, they both wanted to be carried, and I couldn't leave anyone's sight.

"Why can't I do this? Everyone seems to be doing it just fine! What is wrong with me? I can't ask for help. That would make me look weak, and I can't have that!"

It's nine in the evening, and Daniel doesn't come home for another hour. There is a strange odor coming from the kitchen, and both of the girls were so tired, but I wasn't able to soothe both of them at the same time. The girls and I go up to Genevieve's room, and I try my best to get both of them to relax. The lights are dim; I am sitting on the floor with Teresa in my arms while Genevieve is in her crib trying to go to sleep. My mind is running 100 mph, and I just wanted to fall asleep. As I swing Teresa back and forth on the floor, those voices came back.

"You can't do this."

 "You're lucky Daniel doesn't send you away, heck you're lucky if he doesn't divorce you!"

"This is what Sabrina felt before her death. If she couldn't do it, what makes you think you can!"

"Just leave your family. They don't need your burden."

Genevieve was finally asleep in her crib, and I can finally take Teresa to her room next door and try to rock her to sleep. I walk out of Genevieve's room not only feeling exhausted but broken. These thoughts have been running through my mind for months, and they had no intentions in leaving me alone.

It's past 930 pm and pitch dark, as I walk into the hallway, I felt as if someone was watching me. Someone was watching me from the playroom just down the hall. I feel numb and scared because something told me that if I would just look to my left, I might see something that would scare me. The presence, however, felt calm and it was telling me that I will be ok, that this is going to be a painful ride, but I will overcome this. I sighed and wished it were Sabrina. All I wanted was for her to tell me that I will be just fine. I may never know who was with me that night, but I would like to think it was Sabrina; I like to think that she is watching over me especially in those darkest times.

On the nights where I was left alone went on for weeks but I was too afraid to admit to Daniel that I wanted him to stop going to school. What kind of wife would I be if I snatched his dream away from him? He would resent me forever. Teresa was never a good sleeper, and I was sleep deprived and just wanted the pain to go away. It hurt so much that the thought of dying was far more pleasant than being alive!

Towards the end of Daniel's schooling, he knew that I was struggling and he suggested I look for someone to help me on the nights where I was alone, but I was too prideful or felt guilty that I was taking someone else's time to help me! I knew I needed help physically and emotionally, but I was afraid! I was scared to get on medication and have people label me as "The crazy mom!" Since my call at the suicide hotline, I had been going to see a therapist as needed.

Everyone including my therapist knew I needed to see her at least once a week, but I was so afraid of taking time off work. I was losing myself in this dark hell, and I wasn't efficient in my job anymore, which led to an angry boss and co-workers.

"I can't take this anymore! There has got to be a relief for me somewhere! Why can't anyone understand how much this hurts!"

I didn't have time to heal. Everyday was spent taking care of my family and not myself. I can sleep when I'm dead right? A least that is what everyone else was telling me. "I can sleep when I'm dead." Huh. That sounded so pleasant and crazy all at the same time. I became envious of that statement. I would have done anything to get a full night's rest finally and for this

93

heartache to go away! Was the only relief was for me to no longer be here on earth?

Depression was hitting me hard, and I hated life. All I wanted was for someone to tell me that they've felt my pain! I wanted that so much that I searched high and low on the Internet or books of someone who experienced the exact same pain! I couldn't be alone right? I'm not crazy, please someone tell me that I am not crazy!

When I would first meet with my therapist, she would ask if I ever had anxiety attacks. At the time, those attacks looked like a fast heartbeat, sweating palms, and rapid breathing. So, yes, I told myself that I wasn't experiencing any of that or at least not all at once. However, I did mention my anger issues. If I were triggered by something or felt overwhelmed, I would start yelling and acting very irrational to my family.

That is what happened the weekend of Thanksgiving 2016, Daniel and I were arguing about something. We had been doing this for some time now, and none of us was sure how to stop it. That night, when I couldn't yell anymore, I sat in my bedroom alone with my negative thoughts. After sitting for what seemed like forever, those thoughts let me grab my gun and leave the house. I quickly shoved the gun in my purse and left, alone. Once I got to the nearby park, I called a very close friend of mine that understood what if felt like to suffer from depression. I told him the situation, and because he was worried about my well being, he sent the cops to send me to the emergency room.

The officer looked at me and said, "Are you going to be ok?" I wanted so much to lie just so I can go back to my family, but something in my heart just made the truth come out. "I don't know," I reply to him. That was all he needed to hear for him to feel that he should call the ambulance to take me in for a psych evaluation. I had no clue what was about to happen, but because I felt compassion in the officer's voice, I trusted him and trusted the fact that I would be treated the same way once we got to the hospital.

Once the ambulance arrived, the ladies that helped me in were very kind although I felt awkward. "They must think I'm crazy! Look at them looking at me, they think I should be locked up don't they?" The moment we got into the emergency room, the compassion was out the door. We waited for the doctor to come up to me and without even taking me off the gurney, he took one look at me and said, "Not having a good day huh? Well, I am going to send you to the psych ward to be evaluated, and possibly get admitted for a couple of days." He didn't even give me a chance to say one word before he walked away to talk to the next patient.

The lack of compassion was making me feel even worse and also about the fact that I may not know when will be the next time I see my family again! My cries were apparently so loud that the nurse that was leading me into my patient room told me that I needed to stop crying! What the hell is this? I am not a criminal! All of my belongings were taken away from me, and I was left all alone in a room with metal walls! There was nothing on television for me to distract my thoughts. So, I looked up at God and said, "Lord, if you love me, please help out of this darkness!"

After waiting for what seemed like hours, the therapist came in to determine if I should be admitted.

Stay calm Diana. If you overreact, these people wouldn't be afraid to lock you up! The therapist came in, and she was surprisingly very kind! She actually took the time to listen to my story and because of that, I felt that I didn't have to lie my way out of here. After talking for about thirty minutes, she determined that I was no harm to myself; however; she highly recommended that I seek help from a therapist. Since I was already seeing someone that meant that I really needed to follow my treatment plan.

The therapist later discharged me from the hospital and told my nurses to call Daniel and pick me up. Hours later, the Ambien they gave me finally kicked in, and I was woken up by a nurse to let me know that I've been discharged. Daniel came to get me, and it was a quiet ride home. He was concerned and afraid for his wife. No one in my family knew what to do with me. No one. It was the most lonely time of my life. After being in the hospital, my family realized that I've hit rock bottom and this was far bigger than any of us.

The following Monday came along, and all I could think about was where do I go from here? Since the police took my gun, I was concerned about this whole thing would be on my record! Great! Now I'm some kind of criminal, and everyone is going to know I was crazy enough to try to harm myself! Not knowing what to do next, I made sure to make an appointment with my therapist that I have been seeing and move forward with my treatment plan.

I felt so numb that whole week, and I just did not have the momentum to work anymore. There has to be a better way of living. I knew I needed to spend the time to heal but how can I do that if I was working full time and had a family to care for? After much thinking all alone in my own thoughts, I concluded that the only way for me to finally heal was to take some serious time for myself. I asked myself what my most significant stressor was? What is causing me to feel overwhelmed? The answer was simple; it was work and having to be away from my family. There was no time for me to be the mother and wife I wanted to be! I only get one chance at this, and I wanted my girls to grow up knowing that their mother was happy!

That was when I decided to leave my job and start working on myself! No, I didn't have any other plan or any sort of financial replacement. This was probably the worst decision I could make financially, but when I looked at it, it was a matter of life and death. My mental health was worth more than any paycheck. For the first time in my life, I put all my trust in God.

"Ok, Lord, I love you, and I trust you."

Once the day ended, I decided to tell Daniel my plan while we were driving home from work. I probably should have waited until we actually got home, but I am known to never keep a secret for longer than ten minutes! Especially when it was a big deal such as this one! In a timid voice, I tell him that I had to quit my job and if I didn't, I don't know if I would make it out alive. Daniel's reaction was as I expected, as the man of the house, he was worried about our finances. Unfortunately, we were a family that relies on two incomes. Naturally, I was upset by his reaction, but I knew I had to give him time to think about the idea. I told him that I know this is crazy, but I don't know what else to do for me to get better!

It was only after a day when Daniel came around and realized that I was right. This was a matter of life and death, and his love was so powerful that he would do anything for me to get better! Once we both agreed to the plan, it was time for me to tell my boss! Debbie has always been loving and compassionate, but I was afraid to tell her the truth about me. In fact, I didn't want anyone else to know that I was losing my mind! My fear of revealing the truth to her was so intense that I even asked Daniel himself to tell her for me! Daniel would respond, "I can't give her your two weeks notice for you, Diana!" Damn it, I hate it when he's right! He would always do anything for me, but he would never let me be weak! I loved and hated that about him! I never enjoyed being challenged, but he knew that was exactly what I needed.

Later that week, I decided it was time! I stood

up from my chair and walked right into Debbie's office, closed the door, and told her everything. I said that I wasn't coping with Sabrina's death very well and that I had been diagnosed with postpartum depression. I instantly was overwhelmed by the amount of support and concern. She wanted me to get better and knew that it was a matter of life and death! Before I left her office already in tears, she gave me a warm embrace. That was when I knew she would continue to be in my life no matter what!

My Awakening

What was happening to me?

That was the question I would always ask myself. Once I left my day job, I started seeing my therapist every week. She and I were going to peel off the layers of the onion and get to the core of my problems. This was more than Sabrina passing and postpartum depression. There was anger inside that needed to heal. This meant that I had to tell my therapist about my childhood, my pain, and my mistakes. I grabbed the tissue box and started telling her my story. This would take more than one visit! Oh, how I wish I would have more than just an hour!

Growing up, my mother was always angry with the kids especially me. She had three children and most of the time, my father was traveling for work, so she was alone a lot. Looking back and knowing what I do now, I know my mother suffered from postpartum depression and anxiety. Unfortunately, no one including herself was able to recognize, and the damage on her children was done. I was always a rebellious child and always challenged my mother, but since a young child, I remember getting into some intense fights with her up until the day I left the house for good. All the times she would hit me, the angry in me would build up, and I wanted to hit back, but I knew that if I did, I would get hurt even more, so I took my punishment until I was able to run to my room. My elders tell me to respect my parents, but it was difficult for me to do that when I was treated like some dumb kid who didn't know anything. There was one time when I lost all respect for my mother that day.

I was only 8 years old when she betrayed her

family, and after all those years, she never apologized for what I witnessed. What she didn't understand that as an 8-year old, I was a lot smarter than she thought and what she did that day or months fueled my anger for years to come. So many years were spent yelling at her about what she had done, and her response was, "That was in the past! It doesn't matter anymore!" but to me it did, and I carried that pain up until adulthood.

After many arguments with my mother through the years and continually being treated like a child, I decided to move out of the house and live with my then boyfriend. It wasn't the best decision I had ever made, especially since my boyfriend and I were not together for very long, but it was my escape out of this toxic world. I thought that if I didn't leave now, I would never amount to anything in life. I wanted to be on my own but in my parent's culture being on my own meant that I had to get married. So, I got engaged with a man that I was not ready or should be married to. My parents were angry with me, and we didn't talk for weeks after I moved out. I wouldn't be happy at my child either if the only reason why she got engaged were so she can leave the house! In fact, that would break my heart! What my parents didn't see was that my heart was already broken and I've lost all hope in them every trying to repair it! Maybe whoever I marry will fix it! Right? Someone will save me from this! Right?

The only problem to that dream was that the only person that could save me was I! Unfortunately my relationship with my then fiancé did not last and after living with him for only six months, I learned that I was not happy and being with a man that was supposed to "save" me didn't make me happy!

After many sessions with my therapist, we figured out the core to my problems. I needed to start working on forgiving my parents. Yes, they probably will never apologize or realize the pain they've caused, but this wasn't for them. I was letting go for myself so that I may be free from my pain and so that my children can have a mother they deserve and Daniel would have an entirely happy wife!

My anger issues weren't because I "just had a temper" it came from the pain of my childhood, but after becoming a mother myself and the help of my therapist, I learned that they never meant to hurt me! No parent would ever want to harm his or her child intentionally. Were they right for the way I was treated? No, but I realized that it was their own upbringing and all they knew! I was a part of a strict culture where you had to obey your parents until the day you got married! However, the hurt and emotional abuse stop with me and if I wanted my children to live a better life, I had to heal myself first!

Once I found the core to all of my issues that was when I started to heal. I knew my parents love me and now that I am a mother myself, I can finally see the love that they've always had for me. So, the journey to healing started! It was not easy! In fact, it was one painful year for me. I was unpacking every wound I've ever buried and finally started healing from them. This was going to take some time, and all I had was God. No one else was going to help me, It was going to be myself and God's grace that helped me through this.

Choosing Joy

Before losing Sabrina, I was never pleased with myself. Of course, meeting Daniel and building this beautiful family with him made me happy but I wasn't satisfied in my career. I attended college, had decent paying jobs, bought my own car and moved out of my parents. I did everything I thought I needed to do for me to feel successful. But, every night while driving home from work or a late night class, I would cry alone in my car feeling unfulfilled! I had it all and yet, I was still unhappy?

Once I became a mother of two, I quickly grew tired of the hustle and bustle of life. I no longer wanted the "career," I no longer wanted to climb up the ladder or reach for that raise! The only thing I wanted was freedom, freedom to be with my children and go to that dance recital or doctor's appointment without having to ask for permission! The only problem was, how do I get there? We no longer lived in a world where the family can afford one income. It took both Daniel and me to bring enough bacon to the table. I felt as if I was missing out on our children's life. Yes, I was around, but I wasn't present! I was merely surviving and racing through life. My life was always in the fast lane, and I didn't know how to slow down!

When I found out about Sabrina's passing, my life went from 100 mph to a complete stop! She made me realize how short life was and how I was chasing for all the wrong things in life. I was pursuing someone else's dream and not my own. The moment I realized this reality, that was when I went on a journey to find my true identity and finally be able to chase my own dream!

Helping Mothers in a Bigger Way

I didn't have a plan after I left my job, I knew I wanted to start telling stories through a podcast and help moms that felt alone, but I certainly did not come up with a "business plan." All I had was my computer, a mic, and a heart looking for healing! Sabrina was such a fantastic friend in a way that she would put her friends before herself and I felt that she passed a little bit of that to me after she passed. All I wanted was no one else to have to suffer as we did.

When I first started the Always with Me podcast, I was flooded with emails from moms that wanted to share their story! I recorded thirty interviews in thirty days! I do not recommend that by the way! Exhausted was an understatement but I was fascinated by each story I was told! I am a total introvert but this mission pushed me so far out of my comfort zone, I couldn't recognize myself! Who is this happy, confident person? This can't be me! I'm not capable of being an influencer!

After hearing these stories from mothers and many more, I started building powerful, meaningful friendships. It was as if Sabrina knew I was alone and brought this tribe of mothers that were not afraid to be vulnerable! The emails I've received proved that this was where I needed to be. But, I wanted to do more! Why are so many mothers suffering from maternal mental illness? What can I do to prevent the issue?

I started seeing the common denominator; mothers lacked both physical and emotional support. So, again I went to the Internet to see if friends would be able to create a meal train for new moms. Who has time to cook soon after having a baby? This was a great way to help the mother transition into motherhood! That was when a beautiful friend, Lindsay taught me that this was already a thing! They call themselves postpartum doulas! Lindsay found me through a postpartum support group. She heard about my podcast and sent an email about her compelling story! Since our podcast interview, our friendship grew stronger, even if it was only through Facebook! I still had a lot of work to be done on myself, but I knew that postpartum depression was not going to define me; it was going to transform me!

Soon after finding more about what postpartum doulas were, I was shocked that no one ever told me about them! "Why is this not a requirement?" I would say to myself. Every mother, no matter the financial status, needed this type of service. To have the support from someone who was not going to judge your parenting and just to take care of you once you bring baby home? Sign me up, please!

That was when The Always with Me Foundation was born and in honor of my sweet friend, Sabrina! I promised her that no one will suffer as we did ever again! I quickly went on the search on how to create a nonprofit. How in the world will I make this work? I slowly felt Sabrina's embrace and knew she was going to hold my hand through it! It wasn't easy for me to find board members at first. Whom will I trust and who will relate to my mission? All of the mothers I've met I've only known for less than a year! Initially, I had planned to start all of this alone, but the application told me otherwise! I would tell myself, "You can't do this alone like you always do! This was much bigger than you!" That's when I prayed and asked God for his hand in this decision. Thank you,

Lindsay, Jessica, and Sarah for joining me on this journey! I could not have asked for a better team!

My Healing, My self-care

I was on the mission to help moms across the nation but what I forgot about the most, was myself. That seems to be our human nature as women right? We love to help others, but when it came to our needs, that was always last on the list. When was the last time you put yourself on the top of your to-do list? There is some food for thought for you. When was the last time you've taken cared for yourself and tried to heal old wounds?

The hurt from Sabrina's death was not the only hurt I've experienced although definitely one of the most life-changing! That hurt was the one hurt that made me realize that this pain was much more than I thought. Grieving her loss just opened up more of my past heartache and boy was that unpleasant to deal with.

How did I go through all of it? It took a lot of therapy sessions, meditations, podcasts, music, self-help books, writing and so much more! As you can imagine, I've hit many triggers including writing this very book! Sure, I can choose to avoid walking right into my triggers but what would that really do for me? I had to face the pain that I've spent years hiding and learn to let go of the hurt. Let me tell you...letting go of all that baggage never felt more relieving! I learned to forgive those that may have hurt me because really, it was never their intentions to destroy me and if it was then they were just jerks and I didn't need them in my life!

Now, I am not telling you do go knocking on everyone's door and telling them that you forgive them. Although, I guess you could do that but what are the chances of them actually remembering what they've

may have done to your heart? Do you see my point

here? Forgive them for your own mental health!

She Saved Me

The past three years after Sabrina's death has been the most life changing experience and I would have never done anything I've accomplished without her guidance. Although I was not able to save her from the darkest times in life, I like to think that she has saved me and shown me that I am made for so much more.

Since my healing, I've grown The Always with Me Foundation, opened a media production business, and sharing my story all over the world! Although it was not always easy, I've opened my life to so many individuals that shine a light in my darkest days. I don't recognize this life, I was just a mother who spent 40 hours behind a cubicle. I was completely ok with that life but what Sabrina taught me was how life was to short not to live a life you don't love. I've always known I was meant for more, I was intended to create and bring joy to many more individuals.

For the reader that is reading this, I hope I've sparked a fire in your heart, and I challenge you to go after your dreams and be damn good at your skill. Once you've mastered your craft, the money will come. You see, my best friend lost her life and the young age of 26! Life is it not promised and tomorrow may not happen.

To the mother that is reading this, know that you are the best mother for YOUR children and not anyone else! I know what you're thinking. Susie, is doing it better because she posted on social media the batch of cookies she baked for the next PTA meeting that you completely forgot about. That doesn't make you any less of a mother because guess what, we all have our own skills and maybe reading to your children is YOUR thing! Instead of comparing yourself to everyone else and every other mother, love her for who she is because I bet you she is feeling less than, too. When you love your tribe, your tribe will love you back.

To the 18-year-old suffering from depression, it gets better, I promise! I know you've heard this many times before, but it really does. Know that no matter what anyone else tells you, you are beautiful inside and out. God has a plan for you my sweet friend and don't ever let anyone else draw the path to your future. Depression does not define you and I know how hard it can be to wake up in the morning. I know how much you wish just to sleep the pain away! But remember something, when you choose to fight another day, your demons continue to lose!

To the person that just lost someone, put your

hand over your heart, you feel that? You've lived

another day, and I know that empty feeling and Lord I

wish I can bring your person back for you, but they

will always be with you, right in your heart. Continue

to live for them just how I continue to live for Sabrina.

That is what they would want for you! I used to ask

myself if the pain would ever go away and it's been

three years since Sabrina said goodbye, the pain of her

not being here still hurts but what helps to know that

she's always cheering me on. I'll always miss her, but I

know that she doesn't want to see her loved ones crying

over her for the rest of their lives.

When you begin to live a life you love,

everything else just falls into place. So, step out of

your comfort zone and trust the plan God has laid out

for you.

About The Author

Diana Collins is of many things! She is a wife, mother to two beautiful girls, postpartum depression survivor, postpartum doula, president of The Always with Me Foundation, and speaker. She's one busy mama but wouldn't change a thing!

After losing her best friend Sabrina to postpartum depression and hitting rock bottom herself, she went off a journey of healing and finding her purpose in life. She enjoys bringing sisterhood in motherhood and creating authentic relationships wherever she goes.

www.ingramcontent.com/pod-product-compliance
Lightning Source LLC
Chambersburg PA
CBHW031626040426
42452CB00007B/693